Heinemann
InfoSearch

A Rookery of

Penguins

Heinemann Library
Chicago, Illinois

Richard and Louise Spilsbury

Originated by Dot Gradations Ltd
Printed in Hong Kong, China by Wing King Tong

08 07 06 05 04
10 9 8 7 6 5 4 3 2 1

Library of Congress Cataloging-in-Publication Data

Spilsbury, Louise.
  A rookery of penguins / Louise and Richard Spilsbury.
     p. cm. -- (Animal groups)
Summary: Describes the physical characteristics, behavior, habitat, and
group life of penguins.
Includes bibliographical references (p.   ).
  ISBN 1-4034-4691-1 (lib. bdg.) 1-4034-5419-1 (PB)
  1. Penguins--Juvenile literature. [1. Penguins.] I. Spilsbury,
Richard, 1963- II. Title. III. Series.
  QL696.S473S65 2004
  598.47--dc21
                                        2003010348

Acknowledgments

The author and publishers are grateful to the following for permission to reproduce copyright material:

p. 4 Oxford Scientific Films/Kjell Sandved; p. 5 (top) NHPA/David Middleton; p. 5 (bottom) NHPA/Eckart Pott; p. 7 NPL/Peter Bassett; p. 8 Oxford Scientific Films/Ben Osbourne; p. 9 NHPA/Alberto Nardi; pp. 10, 11, 13 (top), 17, 26 NPL/Doug Allan; p. 13 (bottom) NPL/Lynn Stone; p. 14 NHPA/Rod Planck; pp. 14, 22 Guillaume Dargaud; p. 15 National Geographic; p. 16 Still Pictures/Roland Seitre; p. 18 FLPA/Minden Pictures/Tui de Roy; p. 19 NHPA/J. & A. Scott; p. 20 NHPA/Rich Kirchner; p. 21 NHPA/Brian Hawkes; pp. 23, 27 Oxford Scientific Films/Doug Allan; p. 24 (top) Oxford Scientific Films/Daniel Cox; p. 24 (bottom) NHPA/Haroldo Polo; p. 25 Punchstock; p. 28 NHPA/Martin Harvey.

Cover photograph of a group of penguins reproduced with permission of Corbis/Paul A. Souders.

Every effort has been made to contact copyright holders of any material reproduced in this book. Any omissions will be rectified in subsequent printings if notice is given to the publisher.

Contents

Some words are shown in bold, **like this.** You can find out what they mean by looking in the glossary.

What Are Penguins?

Penguins are birds that live by or in the sea most of their lives. There are seventeen different **species,** or kinds, of penguins in the world. Although each species is slightly different, all adult penguins have black backs and white bellies. Like all birds, penguins are animals that have wings, a beak, and bodies covered in feathers. They also lay eggs. Unlike most other birds, penguins cannot fly—although it looks as if they are flying when they swim underwater!

Why can't penguins fly?

Penguins' wings are **adapted** for life in water. They have become narrower, stiffer, and flatter than other bird wings, and the wing feathers are short, so they are not built well for flying. A penguin's wings look more like the flippers of a dolphin, and they help penguins move through water just as a dolphin's flippers do.

Emperor penguins, like this one, are the largest species at over 3 feet (1 meter) tall. The smallest are fairy penguins, which only grow up to 16 inches (41 centimeters).

Do penguins live in groups?

Penguins are some of the most **social** birds in the world. Although penguins spend some time alone, they spend much of their lives with other penguins of the same kind. Penguins form groups to swim and dive, to feed, to travel from one place to another, and also to **breed**. The groups of penguins that form at breeding time are called rookeries.

This is a rockhopper penguin. Its colorful head crest makes it look quite different from other penguins.

Chinstraps are the most common penguin species. They have white faces and a thin black stripe under their chin. They are about 28 inches (70 centimeters) tall.

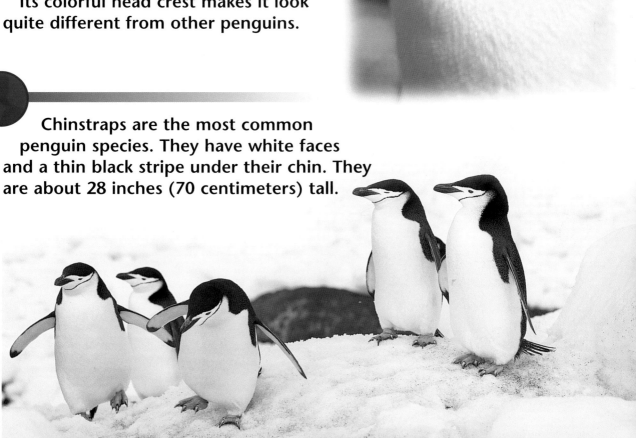

What Is a Rookery?

A rookery of penguins is made up of lots of families. Each family consists of a **male** and **female** pair of adults and their baby penguins. Most male and female penguins look alike. The baby penguins are smaller and covered in fluffy down feathers. Baby penguins are called **chicks.** Penguins gather in rookeries of different sizes. The biggest rookeries number several million penguins, the smallest a few hundred. A rookery almost always contains penguins of only one **species.**

When do rookeries form?

Most penguin species gather on particular areas of land at particular times of year to **breed.** For example, Adélie and chinstrap penguins come ashore in the spring to form their rookeries for a few months. They gather together at this time because it is the best time of year to have and raise young. By the time the young penguins are learning to catch food for themselves, it is summer and there is plenty of food available.

What are rookeries like?

Rookeries are incredibly busy, noisy places. Penguin families argue loudly over nest sites, chicks cry out for food, and parents call to young that have wandered too far. Rookeries also have a strong odor. This is because of the huge amount of **guano** that builds up in the area. People who have visited rookeries say they could smell them long before they could see them!

The largest penguin rookeries in the world can cover as much space as a large town! These are chinstrap penguins in Antarctica.

Do Rookeries Change?

When the **breeding season** is over for the year, most rookeries split up into smaller groups. These smaller groups may spend the rest of the year together in the ocean. For example, king penguins form groups of between five and twenty penguins that swim and feed together. When it is time to **breed** again, all of the smaller groups return to the same place and get together to form large rookeries.

A few **species** of penguin, such as the African penguin, spend their whole lives in rookeries. This is usually because they live in warmer places where young can be born and raised at any time of the year.

Most rookeries, like this rookery of Adélie penguins, break up at the end of the breeding season each year.

Where Do Penguins Live?

All seventeen species of penguins live in the **Southern Hemisphere.** Most penguins live on the coasts of Antarctica or on islands nearby. Some live in warmer places on the coast of South America, Africa, Australia, and New Zealand. For example, Galapagos penguins live on warm **tropical** islands, closer to the **Equator** than any other penguin. Even if they visit warmer shores, all penguins live near cold ocean **currents** because this is where the **prey** that they need to eat lives.

Most of the world's penguins live on or near the icy shores of Antarctica.

For most of the time, penguins are in the sea. Most species of penguins spend at least two-thirds of their lives in water. When they come ashore, penguins live mainly on islands or quiet coastal places where there are few other animals. This is important because the fact that they cannot fly would make them easy prey for **predators.**

Where do rookeries gather?

Rookeries of different **species** gather in different kinds of places. Emperor penguins form rookeries on flat areas of solid ice near the coast, which are sheltered from wind. The small gentoo penguins gather on ice-free ground on beaches and cliffs. Chinstrap rookeries settle on steep, rock-covered slopes. In warmer places, some kinds of penguins, such as the fairy penguin of Australia, make **burrows** to have their young in.

Burrowing penguins, like these Humboldt penguins in Peru, make many burrows close by each other.

What is Antarctica like?

Antarctica has the coldest weather in the world. It is so extremely cold that ice and snow almost always cover the ground. High winds blast across the lower shores, and in winter there are months without daylight. It is a good place for penguins to live because the cold waters contain large amounts of their favorite foods.

How do penguins get around on land?

On land, penguins grip ice or rock with their clawed and **webbed** feet. When penguins walk on their short strong legs, they waddle—they sway back and forth between steps. They may also hop or toboggan if they need to go faster. Tobogganing is when penguins lie on their bellies and push themselves along with their wings. Humans need a sled to toboggan in the snow!

How do they swim in the sea?

Penguins are well **adapted** for swimming in water. They have a **streamlined** shape that makes them look like torpedoes. This helps them shoot through the water fast, with their head tucked back into their neck. Their stiff and paddle-like wings move them along. They use their legs, feet, and tail for steering.

Penguins walk slowly. To move fast on ice, they toboggan along on their bellies!

11

How Do Penguins Survive in the Cold?

The Antarctic is a tough place to live, but the penguins that live there are well **adapted** for survival. They have different features that stop them from getting too cold.

How do penguins keep warm?

Penguins have a thick layer of fat to keep them warm, and their feathers also keep out the cold. Penguins have more feathers than most other birds. Their feathers are also shorter and closer together. The top feathers are **oily** and overlap each other tightly, so they form a warm and waterproof coat. Next to their skin they have short, fluffy feathers that trap a layer of warm air. Their dark back feathers also help absorb or soak up warmth from the sun during the daytime.

On land, penguins keep their wings tight by their sides and tuck their head in their neck to keep warm when standing still. In the water, they stay active and busy to stop themselves from getting too cold.

Do penguins clean their feathers?

Groups of penguins clean their feathers often because they need to keep them in good condition. They use their beaks to spread oil from a **gland** near their tail all over their feathers. This oily coating is what makes the feathers waterproof. If their feathers got wet, the penguins would get very cold and would not survive in Antarctica.

When penguins stand on ice, they tip up their feet so they are resting on their heels and wedge-shaped tail. This reduces the amount of skin that touches the ice, so they stay warmer.

Adult **male** emperor penguins huddle together to protect themselves from the extreme cold and biting winds while they **incubate** their eggs by keeping them warm between their feet.

Do penguins ever lose their feathers?

Once a year, penguins lose their feathers. This is called **molting.** This gets rid of worn-out feathers so strong, new ones can grow in their place. For about two to four weeks during molting a penguin's coat is thin and patchy. During this time, they have no protection in the cold water and cannot swim. That means they cannot feed. Before molting they must eat a lot to store up the extra fat they will use during molting.

New feathers grow up from beneath and push out a penguin's old, worn-out feathers when it molts.

How do penguins keep cool in warm places?

Penguins in warmer places have thinner feathers and a thinner fat layer than penguins in Antarctica. If they get too warm, they move into a shady spot and **pant.** They also hold their wings out in the breeze to cool down. Some, like the fairy penguins of Australia, stay cool at sea during the day. They come ashore in groups in the evening when it is cooler and sleep in **burrows** underground.

What Do Penguins Eat?

Penguins eat mostly small fish, squid, and crabs. They catch and swallow their food whole while they are swimming. Some **species** of penguins prefer particular types of food. For example, Adélie penguins eat mostly krill, which are small, shrimp-like animals. They can swallow up to 2 pounds (1 kilogram) of krill each day!

How far do penguins go to find food?

Different species travel different distances to find food. Some groups of penguins, such as Adélie penguins, feed together in shallow waters near the coast. Others, such as emperor penguins, travel much farther away to look for **prey** in deep waters. In fact, king and emperor penguins may **migrate** over 620 miles (1,000 kilometers) to find large fish and squid.

Some penguins may be away from land feeding for about ten hours at a time, while others may be at sea for days or weeks.

How do penguins catch their food?

Penguins feed mostly during the day. When they spot **prey**, they swim quickly after it. They have good eyesight and they can see better underwater than they can on land. Scientists think that some penguins manage to catch certain types of fish and squid at night because these animals glow in the dark.

Most penguins have a sharp beak that is short and thick and has a strong grip. They also have mouths and tongues lined with little, backward-pointing spines to help them hold on to slippery prey. Some, like the emperor and king penguins, have beaks that curve downward. This helps them catch fast-moving fish and squid in deep waters.

Penguins catch food using their beak. This Adélie penguin's beak has sharp edges to grip fish. The spikes on the inside stop their prey from escaping.

What do penguins drink?

All animals need water to survive. To get water, penguins eat snow and drink fresh water and sea water. Too much salt from sea water could harm their bodies, so they get rid of it through a special **gland** in their beak.

Emperor penguins dive for two to eight minutes. Most dives are within 70 feet (21 meters) of the surface.

How deep can penguins dive?

Most of the prey that penguins eat swims near the surface of the oceans, so they do not have to dive deep to catch it. Penguins cannot breathe underwater, so they must hold their breath while they dive. They usually dive down 65 to 130 feet (20 to 40 meters). Different species dive and swim at different speeds, but most can swim at about 9 miles (14 kilometers) per hour—over twice the speed of the fastest human swimmer!

Do penguins hunt in groups?

Many penguins hunt for food on their own, although close to other penguins from their group, but some kinds of penguins actually work together to catch **prey**.

Groups of Humboldt penguins hunt together for **shoals** of fish such as anchovies and pilchards. When they spot a shoal, the members of the team bob their heads to give the signal to dive together. Then they dive toward the fish from all sides at once, which forces the shoal to form a tight ball. This makes it easy for the penguins to swim straight into the ball to feed. People also have seen emperor penguins working together in this way.

These Galapagos penguins are working as a team to have a better chance of catching enough fish in the sea around the Galapagos Islands.

Do Penguins Talk to Each Other?

Animals in a group **communicate**—pass information to each other—about different things. They may communicate to threaten another penguin or a **predator**, attract a mate to **breed** with, or find their young. Penguins communicate by sound and **displays**.

What sounds do penguins make?

Different **species** of penguins make different kinds of calls. For example, Humboldt penguins make a braying sound like donkeys, chinstraps screech loudly, and king penguins make a trumpeting noise. Individual penguins all sound slightly different, too. This is important for partners to find each other and their **chicks** among hundreds of others in a large rookery. Many penguin groups use a special call at sea to keep in touch with each other. Sound travels well in water—one king penguin can hear another calling from over half a mile (over 1 kilometer) away!

Penguins have excellent hearing and communicate a lot by sound. They hear sounds through small holes just behind their eyes.

What displays do penguins use?

Penguins use **displays** to show how they feel. A display is when an animal does certain things or moves in certain ways to **communicate** with others. Penguins use several different kinds of displays. For example, one kind shows that a particular nest area belongs to them, and another kind frightens off an intruder. A **male** penguin also uses special displays to tell a **female** he wants to breed with her. He may do a lot of head bowing, or wave his wings around. He may also stand up straight with his wings held as far back as he can reach and make a loud wailing sound.

Male Adélie penguins often bring females a gift of a stone. Stones are valuable to these penguins because they use them to build nests. Males give these presents to show they would make a good partner.

How Do Penguins Care for Their Young?

Adult penguins usually return to the rookery site they were born in to **breed.** That is why rookeries become so large. Most females pair up with the same males every year. Young adult penguins have to find a new partner.

What are penguin nests like?

Most penguins make their nests out of piles of grass, moss, mud, stones, or feathers on the ground. Some penguins make nests in **burrows.** Humboldt penguins make burrows in deep piles of their own droppings, called **guano.** The female usually lays two eggs. However, female emperor and king penguins lay only one egg. Different species lay eggs of different sizes and shapes. They may be white, blue, or green. Most penguin parents take turns to **incubate** the eggs. While one sits on the nest, the other goes to sea to feed.

Gentoo penguins make their nests out of all sorts of things, from pebbles to **molted** feathers. Some, like this pair, make their nests out of plants and twigs.

Why do penguins breed in rookeries?

Have you heard the saying, "There is safety in numbers"? Penguins breed in rookeries for that reason—to protect and to defend their young. In a rookery the penguins lay their eggs at roughly the same time so all the **chicks** are about the same age. The many chicks huddle in groups for safety, guarded from **predators** by a few adults, while parents are away at sea finding them food.

Male emperor penguins **incubate** their eggs by holding them close to their bodies, on top of their feet, away from the ice.

Do all penguins make nests?

Emperor and king penguins do not make nests. The males carry a single egg in a flap of skin on their feet. They gather in groups and incubate the eggs for two months while the females are away feeding. The males lose almost half their body weight because they use their body fat as food. When the female returns, it is the male's turn to feed.

What do chicks eat?

At first, parents take turns fetching food for the chicks. They carry fish back in part of their stomach and then regurgitate it, bringing it back up their throat, to feed the chicks. As chicks get bigger, both parents have to go to sea at the same time to get enough food for them.

When do chicks become adults?

Penguin chicks stay with their parents until they have grown a waterproof set of feathers. This takes over a year for king penguins, but for most species, it takes less than ten weeks. With waterproof feathers, the young penguins can go to sea to fetch their own food. Some species of penguin are ready to have young of their own when they are about three years old; other species do not begin to **breed** until they are eight years old.

Young penguins usually peck at their parent's beak and cry out to get their parents to regurgitate food for them.

23

When both parents are away fetching food, older penguin **chicks** huddle together in groups to keep warm and safe. Often, one or two adults stay behind to guard the group from **predators**.

These young chinstrap penguins are **molting** their downy baby feathers, and ready to grow an adult set. Once they have their adult feathers, it is time for the penguins to take care of themselves.

Do Penguins Fight?

When animals live in groups, there are often arguments. **Males** in a rookery argue over finding a **female.** Females and males argue over nest sites and the materials needed to build a nest.

In any disagreement, penguins try to avoid a fight using **displays** to warn an enemy. They might stare at their opponent, or walk toward them in a zig-zag pattern. Some use beak slapping—they shake heads and slap beaks together. If these displays do not work, the penguins fight. Penguins fight beak to beak, by lunging towards each other and pecking or biting. In a large rookery, penguins place their nests as far apart as they can can keep others away while still sitting on their eggs!

These penguins are fighting by slapping their beaks against each other. A penguin's beak is sharp and strong and can cause a lot of damage.

Penguins face many dangers. While they are at sea, many ocean **predators** try to catch and eat penguins. These include leopard seals, sea lions, sharks, and killer **whales.** On land, penguins have few predators, although sea lions sometimes follow them onto land to try to catch them. Rats, dogs, cats, snakes, foxes, and birds, such as skuas, eat eggs and **chicks** if they are left alone by their parents, but these animals would never be able to catch healthy adult penguins.

Leopard seals are one of the penguin's worst enemies.

Why are penguins black and white?

Penguins have black backs and white bellies to help them escape predators when they are in the water. Animals swimming above them find it hard to spot penguins' black backs against the dark waters of deep oceans. Their white bellies make them hard to spot from below, as a predator looks up towards the light sky. This is called **counter-shading.**

How do penguins escape from predators?

Penguins sometimes escape predators by pecking at them, swimming fast, or leaping out of the water and out of reach or onto land. Penguins also call out warnings to others in their group to give them the chance to get away as well.

What else harms penguins?

Many penguins die at sea, usually from starvation. This may be caused by a lack of fish in a particular area, or because bad weather and rough water makes it difficult to catch any. If adults die at sea in the **breeding season**, eggs and chicks back at the rookery will die because they have no one to look after them. Many young penguins die before their first birthday because they have not had enough practice catching fish.

Penguins, like these emperor penguins, can leap almost six and a half feet (two meters) from the water to the safety of a rock or iceberg.

Do people harm penguins?

The biggest danger that penguins face is people. Fishing boats catch so many fish that they make it hard for some penguins to find food. People also cause terrible **pollution** in the oceans. **Oil** dumped or spilled from ships can harm penguins and their nests. Floating garbage can tangle or choke them. In some places, people collect penguin **guano** to use as **fertilizer.** Often, they do not leave enough for the penguins that use guano for their nests, so those penguins do not lay eggs.

Oil can ruin a penguin's feathers, leaving them to freeze to death. These conservation workers are cleaning some oiled penguins they rescued.

Who protects penguins?

In the past there were 32 more **species** of penguin than there are today. These birds, such as the great auk, became **extinct** because of people. Today, only a few penguin species, such as the Galapagos, are **endangered. Conservation** groups are working to protect these penguins so that we do not lose them as well.

Penguin Facts

How do penguins sleep?

Most penguins sleep for a few minutes at a time throughout the day, though they sleep longer at night. At sea they nap sitting in the water. On land they sleep sitting, standing, or lying down. Some sleep with their beak tucked under a wing.

What is a waddle of penguins?

Some people call a group of penguins a waddle of penguins, because of the way they walk.

How long do penguins live?

Healthy penguins can live for up to fifteen years. Larger species of penguin generally live longer—emperor penguins live for twenty years, while rockhoppers live for only ten.

This map shows where different kinds of penguins live in the world.

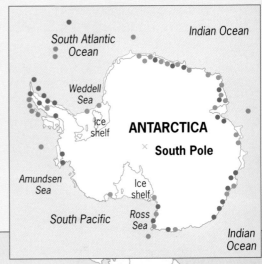

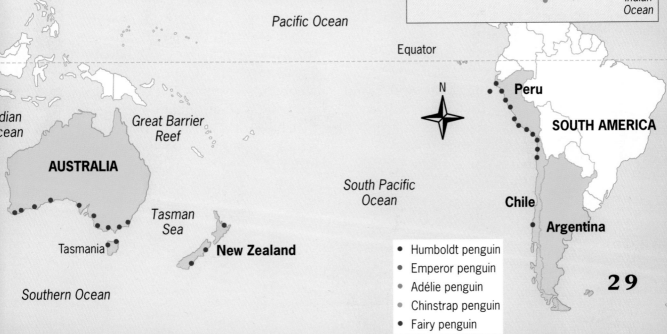

- Humboldt penguin
- Emperor penguin
- Adélie penguin
- Chinstrap penguin
- Fairy penguin

29

Glossary

adapted   when a living thing has special features that allow it to survive in its habitat

breed/breeding   have babies

breeding season   time of the year when a particular type of animal breeds

burrow   below-ground dwelling

chick   young bird

communicate   pass on information

conservation   action to stop wild animals, plants, and places from dying out or being destroyed

counter-shading   form of camouflage in which the animal is a dark color on top and a lighter color underneath

current   stream of water moving through surrounding still water

display   put on a show of actions or movements that sends a message to another animal

endangered   plant or animal in danger of dying out

Equator   imaginary line around the center of the Earth

extinct   when a species has died out and no longer exists

female   animal that, when grown up, can become a mother

fertilizer   something that farmers put on plants to help them grow faster, bigger, or better

gland   part inside an animal's body that makes some of the special chemicals or oils it needs

guano   bird droppings

incubate   keep eggs warm so that the baby inside can grow

male   animal that, when grown up, can become a father

migrate   move to a different place to feed and live for part of the year

molt/molting   when an animal loses its old feathers and grows new ones

oil   greasy substance that does not dissolve in water

pant   breathe with short, quick breaths

pollution   when something poisons or harms the natural world

predator   animal that hunts or catches other animals to eat

prey   animal that is hunted or caught for food by a predator

shoal   group of fish

social   living in a group

Southern Hemisphere   half of the Earth that is south of the Equator

species   group of living things that are similar and can produce healthy offspring together

streamlined   smooth shape that moves through the water easily

tropical   area around the Equator that has a very hot climate

webbed   describes feet of certain animals, such as ducks and penguins, that have skin between their toes

whale   mammal that spends its life in water

More Books to Read

Hall, Margaret. *Penguins and Their Chicks*. Minnetonka, Minn.: Capstone Press, 2003.

Noonan, Diana. *The Emperor Penguin*. Broomall, Penn.: Chelsea House Publishers, 2003.

Raatma, Lucia. *Penguins*. Minneapolis: Compass Point Books, 2001.

Stone, Lynn. *Penguins*. Minneapolis: Lerner Publishing Group, 2002.

Winner, Cherie. *Penguins*. Chanhassen, Minn.: Creative Publishing, International, 2003.

Index